To

From *Dick*

Carol

2003
XMAS

CELEBRATING
America

CELEBRATING
America

A Book of Appreciation

EDITED BY
GLORYA HALE
and S. H. LYNN

MetroBooks

2002 MetroBooks

ISBN 1-58663-599-9

Book design by Rhea Braunstein

Illustrations by Paul Hoffman

Printed and bound in the United States of America

02 03 04 05 06 MC 9 8 7 6 5 4 3 2 1

KP

Introduction

Celebrating America is a tribute to America, a paean to the American spirit and to the American dream. Here in the words of presidents and poets, of writers and statesmen, of historians and artists are the convictions and the ideals that have made America great. Here, too, we see America through foreign eyes. And we become aware once more of the beauty of our country and of the wonderful mosaic of her people. We also hear the voices of men and women who fought and won the battles for equal and civil rights.

This book celebrates those who are determined that our country will always be the home of the free and the brave, a land of opportunity and liberty.

GLORYA HALE

CELEBRATING
America

We, the people of the United States, in order to form a more perfect union, establish justice, insure domestic tranquillity, provide for the common defense, promote the general welfare, and secure the blessings of liberty to ourselves and our posterity, do ordain and establish this Constitution for the United States of America.

Preamble to the Constitution of the United States

It is a noble land that God has given us: a land that can feed and clothe the world; a land whose coastlines would enclose half the countries of Europe; a land set like a sentinel between the two imperial oceans of the globe.

ALBERT J. BEVERIDGE, American politician and historian

The United States themselves are essentially the greatest poem.

WALT WHITMAN, American poet

. . . let me assert my firm belief that the only thing we have to fear is fear itself—nameless, unreasoning, unjustified terror which paralyzes needed efforts to convert retreat into advance.

FRANKLIN D. ROOSEVELT,
32nd president of the United States

We hold these truths to be self-evident, that all men are created equal, that they are endowed by their Creator with certain unalienable rights, that among these are life, liberty, and the pursuit of happiness. That, to secure these rights, governments are instituted among men, deriving their just powers from the consent of the governed.

From the Declaration of Independence, July 4, 1776

If the American Revolution had produced nothing but the Declaration of Independence, it would have been worthwhile.

SAMUEL ELIOT MORISON, American historian

Great harm has been done to us. We have suffered great loss. And in our grief and anger we have found our mission and our moment. Freedom and fear are at war. The advance of human freedom—the great achievement of our time, and the great hope of every time—now depends on us. Our Nation—this generation—will lift a dark threat of violence from our people and our future. We will rally the world to this cause, by our efforts and by our courage. We will not tire, we will not falter, and we will not fail.

GEORGE W. BUSH, 43rd president of the United States

Great spirits have always encountered violent opposition from mediocre minds.

ALBERT EINSTEIN, German-born American physicist

History, despite its wrenching pain,
Cannot be unlived, and if faced
With courage, need not be lived again.

    MAYA ANGELOU, American activist, poet, and screenwriter

Having thus chosen our course, without guile and with pure purpose, let us renew our trust in God, and go forward without fear and with manly hearts.

    ABRAHAM LINCOLN, 16th president of the United States

Give me your tired, your poor,
Your huddled masses yearning to breathe free,
The wretched refuse of your teeming shore.
Send these, the homeless, tempest-tossed, to me,
I lift my lamp beside the golden door!

    EMMA LAZARUS, American poet, essayist, and writer

O beautiful for spacious skies,
For amber waves of grain,
For purple mountain majesties
Above the fruited plain!

America! America!
God shed His grace on Thee,
And crown thy good with brotherhood
From sea to shining sea!

O beautiful for patriot dream
That sees beyond the years
Thine alabaster cities gleam
Undimmed by human tears!

America! America!
God shed His grace on Thee,
And crown thy good with brotherhood
From sea to shining sea!

KATHARINE LEE BATES, American editor and author

We have become not a melting pot but a beautiful mosaic. Different people, different beliefs, different yearnings, different hopes, different dreams.

JIMMY CARTER, 39th president of the United States

America is woven of many strands; I would recognize them and let it so remain. . . . Our fate is to become one, and yet many—This is not prophecy, but description.

RALPH ELLISON, American writer and lecturer

The Stile of this confederacy shall be "The United States of America."

From Articles of Confederation, March 1, 1781

This is a country where a man can stand as a man, and where he can enjoy the fruits of his own exertions, with rational liberty to its fullest extent.

JOHN DOWNE, 19th-century English-born immigrant

France was a land, England was a people, but America, having about it still that quality of the idea, was harder to utter—it was the graves at Shiloh, and the tired, drawn, nervous faces of its great men, and the country boys dying in the Argonne for a phrase that was empty before their bodies withered. It was a willingness of the heart.

From The Crack-Up *by* F. SCOTT FITZGERALD

One flag, one land, one heart, one hand,
One Nation, evermore!

OLIVER WENDELL HOLMES SR.,
American physician, writer, and poet

An American Religion: Work, play, breathe, bathe, study, live, laugh, and love.

ELBERT HUBBARD, *American writer and publisher*

America means opportunity, freedom, power.

> *RALPH WALDO EMERSON, American essayist and poet*

Education, then, beyond all other devices of human origin, is the great equalizer of the conditions of men—the balance wheel of the social machinery.

> *HORACE MANN, educator and president of Antioch College*

May our country be always successful, but whether successful or otherwise, always right.

> *JOHN QUINCY ADAMS, 6th president of the United States*

Thank God we're living in a country where the sky's the limit, the stores are open late and you can shop in bed thanks to television.

> *JOAN RIVERS, American comedian and television personality*

One loves America above all things, for her youth, her greenness, her plasticity, innocence, good intentions, friends, everything.

WILLIAM JAMES, American philosopher and psychologist

Only in America could a refugee girl from Europe become Secretary of State.

MADELEINE ALBRIGHT, Czechoslovakian-born
American secretary of state

We are the standard-bearers in the only really authentic revolution, the democratic revolution against tyrannies. Our strength is not to be measured by our military capacity alone, by our industry, or by our technology. We will be remembered, not for the power of our weapons, but for the power of our compassion, our dedication to human welfare.

HUBERT H. HUMPHREY, 38th vice president of the United States

I do believe we shall continue to grow, to multiply and prosper until we exhibit an association powerful, wise, and happy beyond what has yet been seen by men.

THOMAS JEFFERSON, 3rd president of the United States

The United States is the only great and populous nation-state and world power whose people are not cemented by ties of blood, race, or original language. It is the only world power which recognizes but one nationality of its citizens—American.

DOROTHY THOMPSON, American writer and journalist

OR RELIGION

We go forth all to see America. And in the seeking we create her. In the quality of our search shall be the nature of the America that we created.

WALDO FRANK, American writer

She that lifts up the manhood of the poor,
She of the open soul and open door,
With room about her hearth for all mankind!

JAMES RUSSELL LOWELL, American poet

The forests of America, however slighted by man, must have been a great delight to God, because they were the best He ever planted.

JOHN MUIR, American naturalist

For this is what America is all about. It is the uncrossed desert and the unclimbed ridge. It is the star that is not reached and the harvest that is sleeping in the unplowed ground.

LYNDON B. JOHNSON, 36th president of the United States

Whatever America hopes to bring to pass in the world must first come to pass in the heart of America.

DWIGHT D. EISENHOWER, American general and 34th president of the United States

America is not just a power: it is a promise. It is not
enough for our country to be extraordinary in might; it
must be exemplary in meaning. Our honor and our role
in the world finally depend on the living proof that we are
a just society.

NELSON ROCKEFELLER, *American politician*

Who is the United States? Not the judiciary; not the President; but the sovereign power of the people, exercised
through their representatives in Congress, with the con-
currence of the executive. —NOT LATELY

THADDEUS STEVENS, *American politician*

The American people have encountered together great
dangers and sustained severe trials with success. They con-
stitute one great family with a common interest.

JAMES MONROE, *5th president of the United States*

My country, 'tis of thee,

Sweet land of liberty,

Of thee I sing;

Land where my fathers died;

Land of the pilgrims' pride,

From every mountain side

Let freedom ring.

SAMUEL FRANCIS SMITH,
American clergyman and writer

All I want is the same thing you want. To have a nation with a government that is as good and honest and decent and competent and compassionate and as filled with love as are the American people.

JIMMY CARTER, 39th president of the United States

Oh, it's home again, and home again, America for me!
I want a ship that's westward bound to plough the rolling sea,
To the blessed Land of Room Enough beyond the ocean bars,
Where the air is full of sunlight and the flag is full of stars.

HENRY VAN DYKE, American clergyman, poet, and writer

America is a land of wonders, in which everything is in constant motion and every change seems an improvement.

ALEXIS DE TOCQUEVILLE, French social philosopher

All my childhood I had dressed like an American, eaten American food, and befriended American children. I had gone to an American school and spent most of the day speaking and reading English. At night, my prayers were full of blond hair and blue eyes and snow. All my childhood I had longed for this moment of arrival. And here I was, an American girl, coming home at last.

Julia Alvarez, Dominican-born American
novelist, poet, and educator

Ours has become a nation too great to offend the least, too mighty to be unjust to the weakest, too lofty and noble to be ungenerous to the poorest and lowliest.

Stephen Wise, American rabbi and writer

It has been the true glory of the United States to cultivate peace by observing justice.

James Madison, 4th president of the United States

I always consider the settlement of America with reverence and wonder, as the opening of a grand scene and design in providence, for the illumination of the ignorant and the emancipation of the slavish part of mankind all over the earth.

JOHN ADAMS, 2nd president of the United States

Of all the nations in the world, the United States was built in nobody's image. It was the land of the unexpected, of unbounded hope, of ideals, of quest for an unknown perfection.

DANIEL J. BOORSTIN, American historian

America is rather like life. You can usually find in it what you look for. . . . It will probably be interesting, and it is sure to be large.

E.M. FORSTER, British novelist and essayist

Ours is the only country deliberately founded on a good idea.

JOHN GUNTHER, American journalist

Lo, body and soul—this land,
My own Manhattan with spires, and the sparkling and
    hurrying tides, and the ships,
The varied and ample land, the South and the North in
    the light, Ohio's shores and flashing Missouri,
And ever the far-spreading prairies cover'd with grass
    and corn.

WALT WHITMAN, American poet

No author, without a trial, can conceive of the difficulty
of writing a romance about a country where there is no
shadow, no antiquity, no mystery, no picturesque and
gloomy wrong, nor anything but a commonplace prosper-
ity, in broad and simple daylight, as is happily the case with
my dear native land.

NATHANIEL HAWTHORNE, American writer and statesman

I feel most at home in the United States, not because it is intrinsically a more interesting country, but because no one really belongs there any more than I do.

  WYNDHAM LEWIS, American-born English painter and writer

It is capitalist America that produced the modern independent woman. Never in history have women had more freedom of choice in regard to dress, behavior, career, and sexual orientation.

    CAMILLE PAGLIA, American writer, critic, and educator

America is a nation created by all the hopeful wanderers of Europe, not out of geography and genetics, but out of purpose.

    THEODORE H. WHITE, American journalist and writer

That land is like an Eagle, whose young gaze
Feeds on the noontide beam, whose golden plume
Floats moveless on the storm, and in the blaze
Of sunrise gleams when Earth is wrapped in gloom;
An epitaph of glory for the tomb
Of murdered Europe may thy fame be made,
Great People! As the sands shalt though become;
Thy growth is swift as morn, when night must fade;
The multitudinous Earth shall sleep beneath thy shade.

PERCY BYSSHE SHELLEY, English poet

America is a vast conspiracy to make you happy.

JOHN UPDIKE, American writer

America lives in the heart of every man everywhere who wishes to find a region where he will be free to work out his destiny as he chooses.

WOODROW WILSON, 28th president of the United States

My country is the world, and my religion is to do good.

THOMAS PAINE, Revolutionary patriot, philosopher, and writer

I would rather . . . have a nod from an American, than a snuff-box from an emperor.

GEORGE GORDON, LORD BYRON, English poet

The Americans have none of the irony of the English, none of their cool poise, none of their manner. But they do have friendliness. Where an Englishman would give you his card, an American would very likely give you his shirt.

RAYMOND CHANDLER, American writer

There is one thing that America knows well, and that she teaches as a great and precious lesson to those who come into contact with her amazing adventure: that is the value and dignity of the man of common humanity, the value and dignity of the people.

JACQUES MARITAIN, French philosopher

It is, I believe, the destiny of America to produce the first of a new species of man.

WYNDHAM LEWIS, American-born English painter and writer

Nothing is impossible in the United States.

EVE CURIE, French writer

That on the first day of January, in the year of Our Lord one thousand eight hundred and sixty-three, all persons held as slaves within any state, or designated part of a state, the people whereof shall then be in rebellion against the United States, shall be then, thenceforward, and forever free; and the executive government of the United States, including the military and naval authority thereof, will recognize and maintain the freedom of such persons, and will do no act or acts to repress such persons, or any of them, in any efforts they may make for their actual freedom.

From The Emancipation Proclamation

America is full of a violent desire to learn.

Le Corbusier, French architect

I shall use the words America and democracy as convertible terms.

Walt Whitman, American poet

The American lives even more for his goals, for the future, than the European. Life for him is always becoming, never being.

Albert Einstein, German-born American physicist

They are not men, they are not women, they are Americans.

Pablo Picasso, Spanish artist

I am still very much of an American. That is to say, naïve, optimistic, gullible. . . . Like it or not, I am a product of this land of plenty, a believer in super-abundance, a believer in miracles.

HENRY MILLER, American expatriate writer

I got into the car and lit out to drift for a time. I had a grand ride, over mountains and rivers and out onto the prairies, crossed the Cumberland, Tennessee, Ohio, Mississippi, and Missouri Rivers. It rained, the wind blew and the sun shone. Again I got in love with America. What a land!

SHERWOOD ANDERSON, American writer

We are a nation of communities, of tens and tens of thousands of ethnic, religious, social, business, labor union, neighborhood, regional and other organizations, all of them varied, voluntary, and unique . . . a brilliant diversity spread like stars, like a thousand points of light in a broad and peaceful sky.

GEORGE BUSH, 41st president of the United States

I fell in love with my country—its rivers, prairies, forests, mountains, cities, and people. No one can take my love of country away from me! I felt then, as I do now, it's a rich, fertile, beautiful land, capable of satisfying all the needs of its people.

ELIZABETH GURLEY FLYNN, American labor organizer

In the United States there is more space where nobody is than where anybody is. That is what makes America what it is.

GERTRUDE STEIN, American expatriate writer

Make no mistake; the American Revolution was not fought to *obtain* freedom, but to *preserve* the liberties that Americans already had as colonials. Independence was no conscious goal, secretly nurtured in cellar or jungle by bearded conspirators, but a reluctant last resort, to preserve "life, liberty, and the pursuit of happiness."

SAMUEL ELIOT MORISON, American historian

And so, my fellow Americans: ask not what your country can do for you—ask what you can do for your country.

JOHN F. KENNEDY,
35th president of the United States

I think of a hero as someone who understands the degree of responsibility that comes with his freedom.

BOB DYLAN, American singer and songwriter

Our whole duty, for the present at any rate, is summed up in the motto: America first.

WOODROW WILSON, 28th president of the United States

It is not simple to be an American.

HENRY JAMES, American expatriate writer

Our flag is red, white, and blue, but our nation is a rainbow—red, yellow, brown, black, and white—and we're all precious in God's sight. America is not like a blanket—one piece of unbroken cloth, the same color, the same texture, the same size. America is more like a quilt—many patches, many pieces, many colors, many sizes, all woven and held together by a common thread.

JESSE JACKSON, American clergyman and civil rights leader

A President's hardest task is not to do what is right, but to know what is right.

LYNDON B. JOHNSON, 36th president of the United States

To risk your life for a total stranger in need is not only courageous, but divine, because in the face of that kind of selflessness we can no longer call each other strangers. That is brotherhood. That is America.

JIM CARREY, Canadian-born actor

One cannot be an American by going about saying that one is an American. It is necessary to feel America, like America, love America, and then work.

GEORGIA O'KEEFFE, American artist

These are the times that try men's souls. The summer soldier and the sunshine patriot will, in this crisis, shrink from the service of their country; but he that stands it *now,* deserves the love and thanks of men and women.

THOMAS PAINE, Revolutionary patriot, philosopher, and writer

I love and admire the American soldier, and think him equal, if not the superior, of any warrior of any time. He is not only brave but he has no desire to crush his foe, but is eager to abide by the old Latin maxim of "live and let live," and he forgets and forgives, and lends a helping hand when a disposition to do the right thing is shown.

*CLARA BARTON, American nurse and
founder of the American Red Cross*

I must study politics and war that my sons may have liberty to study mathematics and philosophy.

JOHN ADAMS, 2nd president of the United States

Then join hand in hand, brave Americans all,
By uniting we stand, by dividing we fall.

> *JOHN DICKINSON, Revolutionary patriot and essayist*

If we wish to be free; if we mean to preserve inviolate those inestimable privileges for which we have been so long contending; if we mean not basely to abandon the noble struggle in which we have been so long engaged, and which we have pledged ourselves never to abandon until the glorious object of our contest shall be obtained—we must fight!

> *PATRICK HENRY, American Revolutionary leader*

The making of an American begins at that point where he himself rejects all other ties, any other history, and himself adopts the vesture of his adopted land.

> *JAMES BALDWIN, American writer*

Nothing so challenges the American spirit as tackling the biggest job on earth. . . . Americans are stimulated by the big job—the Panama Canal, Boulder Dam, Grand Coulee, Lower Colorado River developments, the tallest building in the world, the mightiest battleship.

LYNDON B. JOHNSON, 36th president of the United States

By the rude bridge that arched the flood,
Their flag to April's breeze unfurled,
Here once the embattled farmers stood,
And fired the shot heard round the world.

RALPH WALDO EMERSON, American essayist and poet

America excited an admiration that must be felt on the spot to be understood.

JAMES BRYCE, British historian, diplomat, and jurist

Examples to the contrary notwithstanding, the essence of the United States is to be found in its small towns. This cannot be said of any other country . . . The American village . . . is a small edition of the whole country, in its civil government, its press, its schools, its banks, its town hall, its census, its spirit, and its appearance.

DOMINGO FAUSTINO SARMIENTO, Argentine political leader

This will remain the land of the free only so long as it is the home of the brave.

ELMER DAVIS, American writer and radio commentator

The next year, the next decade, in all likelihood the next generation, will require more bravery and wisdom on our part than any period in our history. We will be face to face, every day, in every part of our lives and times, with the real issue of our age—the issue of survival.

JOHN F. KENNEDY, 35th president of the United States

We have seen the state of our Union in the endurance of rescuers, working past exhaustion. We have seen the unfurling of flags, the lighting of candles, the giving of blood, the saying of prayers—in English, Hebrew, and Arabic. We have seen the decency of a loving and giving people who have made the grief of strangers their own. My fellow citizens, for the last nine days, the entire world has seen for itself the state of our Union—and it is strong.

GEORGE W. BUSH, 43rd president of the United States

A democracy is peace loving. It does not like to go to war. It is slow to rise to provocation. When it has once been provoked to the point where it must grasp the sword, it does not easily forgive its adversary for having produced this situation. The fact of the provocation then becomes itself the issue. Democracy fights in anger—it fights for the very reason that it was forced to go to war.

GEORGE F. KENNAN, American diplomat and historian

A vigorous democracy—a democracy in which there are freedom from want, freedom from fear, freedom of religion, and freedom of speech—would never succumb to communism or any other ism.

HELEN GAHAGAN DOUGLAS,
American actor and congresswoman

Driven from every other corner of the earth, freedom of thought and the right of private judgment in matters of conscience direct their course to this happy country as their last asylum.

SAMUEL ADAMS, Revolutionary patriot and statesman

Freedom of expression is the matrix, the indispensable condition, of nearly every other form of freedom.

BENJAMIN N. CARDOZO, Associate Justice of the
United States Supreme Court

The first requisite of a good citizen in this Republic of ours is that he shall be able and willing to pull his weight.

THEODORE ROOSEVELT, 26th president of the United States

The beauty of a democracy is that you never can tell when a youngster is born what he is going to do with himself; and that no matter how humbly he is born, no matter where he is born, no matter what circumstances hamper him at the outset, he has got a chance to master the minds and lead the imagination of the whole country.

WOODROW WILSON, 28th president of the United States

What is freedom? Freedom is the right to choose: the right to create for oneself the alternatives of choice. Without the possibility of choice and the exercise of choice a man is not a man but a member, an instrument, a thing.

ARCHIBALD MACLEISH, American poet and dramatist

As long as men are free to ask what they must, free to say what they think, free to think what they will, freedom can never be lost, and science can never regress.

J. ROBERT OPPENHEIMER, American physicist

I love America more than any other country in this world, and exactly for this reason, I insist on the right to criticize her perpetually.

JAMES BALDWIN, American writer

We must not confuse dissent with disloyalty.

EDWARD R. MURROW,
American news reporter and commentator

We are constantly thinking of the great war . . . which saved the Union . . . but it was a war that did a great deal more than that. It created in this country what had never existed before—a national consciousness. It was not the salvation of the Union, it was the rebirth of the Union.

WOODROW WILSON, 28th president of the United States

Once I thought to write a history of the immigrants in America. Then I discovered that the immigrants *were* American history.

OSCAR HANDLIN, American historian and educator

We are a nation of immigrants. It is immigrants who brought to this land the skills of their hands and brains to make of it a beacon of opportunity and of hope for all men.

HERBERT H. LEHMAN, American banker and politician

You can only protect your liberties in this world by protecting the other man's freedom. You can only be free if I am free.

CLARENCE DARROW, American lawyer

A patriot is one who wrestles for the
soul of her country
as she wrestles for her own being.

> *ADRIENNE RICH, American poet and educator*

Liberty without learning is always in peril and learning
without liberty is always in vain.

> *JOHN F. KENNEDY, 35th president of the United States*

The strongest government on earth I believe is the only
one where every man, at the call of the law, would fly to
the standard of the law, and would meet invasions of the
public order as his own personal concern.

> *THOMAS JEFFERSON, 3rd president of the United States*

America is a nation full of good fortune, with so much to be grateful for. But we are not spared from suffering. In every generation, the world has produced enemies of human freedom. They have attacked America, because we are freedom's home and defender. And the commitment of our fathers is now the calling of our time.

GEORGE W. BUSH, 43rd president of the United States

I had forgotten how rich and beautiful is the country-side—the deep topsoil, the wealth of great trees, the lake country of Michigan handsome as a well-made woman, and dressed and jeweled. It seemed to me that the earth was generous and outgoing here in the heartland, and per-haps the people took a cue from it.

JOHN STEINBECK, American writer

I like the dreams of the future better than the history of the past.

THOMAS JEFFERSON, 3rd president of the United States

There is in the American mind, just because it *is* an American mind, an idealism that cannot be quenched, a small voice of conscience that all the hokum in the world cannot drown.

J.B. PRIESTLEY, English writer

The only soil in which liberty can grow is that of a united people. We must have faith that the welfare of one is the welfare of all. We must know that the truth can only be reached by the expression of our free opinions, without fear and without rancor. . . . We must learn to abhor those disruptive pressures, whether religious, political, or economic, that the enemies of liberty employ.

WENDELL WILKIE, American lawyer,
politician, and business executive

Let us by all wise and constitutional measures promote intelligence among the people as the best means of preserving our liberties.

JAMES MONROE, 5th president of the United States

The name of American, which belongs to you in your national capacity, must always exalt the just pride of patriotism more than any appellation derived from local discriminations.

GEORGE WASHINGTON, *commander in chief of the Continental Army and 1st president of the United States*

Let our object be, our country, our whole country, and nothing but our country.

DANIEL WEBSTER, *American lawyer and statesman*

I venture to suggest that patriotism is not a short and frenzied outburst of emotion but the tranquil and steady dedication of a lifetime.

ADLAI E. STEVENSON, *American politician and statesman*

A nation is formed by the willingness of each of us to share in the responsibility for upholding the common good.

BARBARA JORDAN, *American congresswoman and educator*

No man should think that peace comes easily. Peace does not come by merely wanting it, or shouting for it, or marching down Main Street for it. Peace is built brick by brick, mortared by the stubborn effort and the total energy and imagination of able and dedicated men. And it is built in the living faith that, in the end, man can and will master his own destiny.

LYNDON B. JOHNSON, 36th president of the United States

To be prepared for war is one of the most effective means of preserving peace.

GEORGE WASHINGTON, commander in chief of the Continental Army and 1st president of the United States

If there must be trouble, let it be in my day, that my child may have peace.

THOMAS PAINE, Revolutionary patriot, philosopher, and writer

It isn't enough to talk about peace. One must believe in it. And it isn't enough to believe in it. One must work at it.

ELEANOR ROOSEVELT,
American first lady and writer

The peace we seek is nothing less than the fulfillment of our whole faith among ourselves and in our dealings with others. This signifies more than the stilling of guns, easing the sorrow of war. More than an escape from death, it is a way of life. More than a haven for the weary, it is a hope for the brave.

> *DWIGHT D. EISENHOWER, American general and*
> *34th president of the United States*

Whoever wants to know the heart and mind of America had better learn baseball, the rules and realities of the game—and do it by watching first some high school and small-town teams.

JACQUES BARZUN, French-born American writer and historian

The American Constitution, one of the few modern political documents drawn up by men who were forced by the sternest circumstances to think out what they really had to face, instead of chopping logic in a university classroom.

> *GEORGE BERNARD SHAW, Irish playwright*

America, with the same voice which spoke herself into existence as a nation, proclaimed to mankind the inextinguishable rights of human nature, and the only lawful foundation of government.

JOHN QUINCY ADAMS, 6th president of the United States

Let every nation know, whether it wishes us well or ill, that we shall pay any price, bear any burden, meet any hardship, support any friend, oppose any foe to assure the survival and the success of liberty.

JOHN F. KENNEDY, 35th president of the United States

Here individuals of all nations are melted into a new race of men, whose labors and posterity will one day cause great changes in the world.

MICHEL GUILLAUME JEAN DE CRÈVECOEUR,
French-born Colonial writer

Here is not merely a nation but a teeming nation of nations.

WALT WHITMAN, American poet

Two things in America are astonishing: the changeableness of most human behavior and the strange stability of certain principles. Men are constantly on the move, but the spirit of humanity seems almost unmoved.

ALEXIS DE TOCQUEVILLE, French social philospher

Four score and seven years ago our fathers brought forth, upon this continent, a new nation, conceived in liberty, and dedicated to the proposition that all men are created equal.

ABRAHAM LINCOLN, 16th president of the United States

Democracy is not a spectator sport.

MARIAN WRIGHT EDELMAN, American lawyer and founder of the Children's Defense Fund

I hear America singing, the varied carols I hear,
Those of mechanics, each one singing his as it should be
blithe and strong,
The carpenter singing his as he measures his plank or
beam,
The mason singing his as he makes ready for work, or
leaves off work,
The boatman singing what belong to him in his boat,
The deckhand singing on the steamboat deck,
The shoemaker singing as he sits on his bench, the hatter
singing as he stands,
The wood-cutter's song, the ploughboy's on his way in
the morning, or at noon intermission or at sundown,
The delicious singing of the mother, or of the young
wife at work, or of the girl sewing or washing,
Each singing what belongs to him or her and to none
else,
The day what belongs to the day—at night the party of
young fellows, robust, friendly,
Singing with open mouths their strong, melodious songs.

WALT WHITMAN, American poet

There are two kinds of restrictions upon human liberty—
the restraint of law and that of custom. No written law has
ever been more binding than unwritten custom supported
by popular opinion.

CARRIE CHAPMAN CATT,
American suffragist, educator, and journalist

We look for a younger generation that is going to be more
American than we are. We are doing the best that we can, and
yet we can do better than that, we can do more than that, by
inculcating in the boys and girls of this country today some
of the underlying fundamentals, the reasons that brought our
immigrant ancestors to this country, the reasons that impelled
our revolutionary ancestors to throw off a fascist yoke.

FRANKLIN D. ROOSEVELT,
32nd president of the United States

Here in America, where our society is based on belief in the individual, not contempt for him, the free principle of life has a chance of surviving. I believe that it must and will survive. To understand freedom is an accomplishment which all men may acquire who set their minds in that direction; and to love freedom is a tendency which many Americans are born with. To live in the same room with freedom, or in the same hemisphere, is still a profoundly shaking experience for me.

E.B. WHITE, American writer, humorist, and satirist

Some of us have chosen America as the land of our adoption; the rest have come from those who did the same. For this reason we have some right to consider ourselves a picked group, a group of those who had the courage to break from the past and brave the dangers and the loneliness of a strange land. What was the object that nerved us, or those that went before us, to this choice? We sought liberty; freedom from oppression, freedom from want, freedom to be ourselves.

LEARNED HAND, American judge

And what are we?

We, the people without a race,

Without a language;

Of all races, and of none;

Of all tongues, and one imposed;

Of all traditions and all pasts,

With no tradition and no past.

A patchwork and an

altar-piece. . . .

AMY LOWELL,
American poet

Those of us who shout the loudest about Americanism in making character assassinations are all too frequently those who, by our own words and acts, ignore some of the basic principles of Americanism—

The right to criticize.

The right to hold unpopular beliefs.

The right to protest.

The right of independent thought.

MARGARET CHASE SMITH,
American congresswoman and senator

"Duty," "honor," "country"—these three hallowed words reverently dictate what you want to be, what you can be, what you will be. They are your rallying point to build courage when courage seems to fail, to regain faith when there seems to be little cause for faith, to create hope when hope becomes forlorn.

DOUGLAS MACARTHUR, American general

From the halls of Montezuma
To the shores of Tripoli;
We fight our country's battles
On the land as on the sea;
First to fight for right and freedom
And to keep our honor clean;
We are proud to claim the title
Of United States Marines.

Author Unknown

What we need in the United States is not division; what we need in the United States is not hatred; what we need in the United States is not violence or lawlessness, but love and wisdom, and compassion toward one another, and a feeling of justice towards those who still suffer within our country, whether they be white or they be black.

ROBERT F. KENNEDY, American attorney general and senator

America has its faults as a society, as we have ours. But I think of the Union of America born out of the defeat of slavery. I think of its Constitution, with its inalienable right to every citizen still a model for the world. I think of a black man, born in poverty, who became Chief of their Armed Forces and is now Secretary of State—Colin Powell—and I wonder frankly whether such a thing could have happened here. I think of the Statue of Liberty and how many refugees, migrants, and the impoverished passed its light and felt if not for them, for their children, a new world could indeed be theirs. I think of a country where people who do well, don't have questions asked about their accent, their class, their beginning, but have admiration for what they have done and the success they've achieved. . . .

TONY BLAIR, *prime minister of Great Britain*

Of all nationalities, Americans are the best in adapting themselves.

JENNIE JEROME CHURCHILL, *American-born English writer*

All other nations had come into being among people whose families had lived for time out of mind on the same land where they were born. Englishmen are English, Frenchmen are French. Chinese are Chinese, while their governments come and go; their national states can be torn apart and remade without losing their nationhood. But Americans are a nation born of an idea; not the place, but the idea, created the United States Government.

THEODORE H. WHITE,
American journalist, essayist, and historian

Sometimes people call me an idealist. Well, that is the way I know I am an American. . . . America is the only idealist nation in the world.

WOODROW WILSON, 28th president of the United States

There seemed to be nothing to see; no fences, no creeks or trees, no hills or fields. If there was a road, I could not make it out in the faint starlight. There was nothing but land: not a country at all, but the material out of which countries are made.

From My Antonia *by* WILLA CATHER

My father's folks came from Austria; where did your father's folks come from? From somewhere else, not here. Even if you're a full-blooded Cherokee, it's commonly accepted that your folks immigrated to America from somewhere else—on foot across a land bridge from Asia, maybe—and the rest of us got here in steerage from Liverpool or in tourist class from San Juan or in chains from the Ivory Coast. They have opened Ellis Island to tourists, which means that the place where sixteen million strangers in fur hats and babushkas came knocking at the golden door may now be visited by their grandchildren wearing flowered shirts with cameras around their necks. It is an occasion for remembering that we all came from somewhere else.

CHARLES KURALT, American writer and television journalist

My literary agenda begins by acknowledging that America has transformed *me*. It does not end until I show how I (and the hundreds of thousands like me) have transformed America.

BHARATI MUKHERJEE, Indian-born American novelist

My definition of a free society is a society where it is safe to be unpopular.

ADLAI E. STEVENSON, American politician and statesman

The American destiny is what our fathers dreamed, a land of the free, and the home of the brave; but only the brave can be free. Science has made the dream of today's reality for all the earth if we have the courage and vision to build it. American Democracy must furnish the engineers of world plenty—the builders of world peace and freedom.

MARIAN LA SUEUR, social and political activist

I do not mistrust the future.

BENJAMIN HARRISON, 23rd president of the United States

So at last I was going to America! Really, really going, at last! The boundaries burst. The arch of heaven soared. A million suns shone out of every star. The winds rushed out into outer space, roaring in my ears, "America! America!"

From The Promised Land *by MARY ANTIN*

The Nation believes thoroughly in an honorable peace under which the rights of its citizens are to be everywhere protected.

CALVIN COOLIDGE, 30th president of the United States

A democratic form of government, a democratic way of life, presupposes free public education over a long period; it presupposes also an education for personal responsibility that too often is neglected.

ELEANOR ROOSEVELT, American first lady and writer

America is the only idealist nation in the world.

WOODROW WILSON, 28th president of the United States

Liberty cannot be caged into a charter and handed on ready made to the next generation. Each generation must re-create liberty for its own times. Whether or not we establish freedom rests with ourselves.

FLORENCE ELLINWOOD ALLEN,
American writer, lawyer, and judge

These [country women] are women of the American soil. They are a hard stock. They are the roots of our country. . . . They live with courage and purpose, a part of our tradition.

DOROTHEA LANGE, American photographer

[America] created in me a yearning for all that is wide and open and expansive. Something that will never allow me to fit in in my own country, with its narrow towns and narrow roads and narrow kindnesses and narrow reprimands.

ANTHONY HOPKINS, Welsh actor

America is not only the cauldron of democracy, but the incubator of democratic principles.

MADAME CHIANG KAI-SHEK,
Chinese reformer, educator, and sociologist

Let me assure my countrymen of the Southern States that it is my earnest desire to regard and promote their truest interest—the interests of the white and of the colored people both and equally—and to put forth my best efforts in behalf of a civil policy which will forever wipe out in our political affairs the color line and the distinction between North and South, to the end that we may have not merely a united North or a united South, but a united country.

RUTHERFORD B. HAYES, 19th president of the United States

Yes, we have a good many poor tired people here already, but we have plenty of mountains, rivers, woods, lots of sunshine and air, for tired people to rest in. We have Kansas wheat and Iowa corn and Wisconsin cheese for them to eat, Texas cotton that they can wear. So give us as many as come—we can take it, and take care of them.

MARY MARGARET MCBRIDE,
American writer and radio personality

You people of the United States of America have the wonderfully farseeing conception of being Democracy's material and spiritual arsenal, to save the world's highest values from annihilation.

QUEEN JULIANA, Queen of the Netherlands

WW II

The passion for freedom is on the rise. Tapping this new spirit, there can be no nobler nor more ambitious task for America to undertake . . . than to help shape a just and peaceful world that is truly humane.

JIMMY CARTER, 39th president of the United States

I ran [for President of the United States] because someone had to do it first. In this country everyone is supposed to be able to run for President, but that's never really been true. I ran *because* most people think the country isn't ready for a black candidate, not ready for a woman candidate. Some day . . .

SHIRLEY CHISHOLM,
American writer, educator, and congresswoman

We have every right to dream heroic dreams. Those who say that we are in a time when there are no heroes just don't know where to look. You can see heroes every day going in and out of factory gates. Others, a handful in numbers, produce enough food to feed all of us and then the world beyond. You meet heroes across a counter—and they are on both sides of that counter. . . . They are individuals and families whose taxes support the Government and whose voluntary gifts support church, charity, culture, art, and education. Their patriotism is quiet but deep. Their values sustain our national life.

RONALD REAGAN, 40th president of the United States

Rhetoric is a poor substitute for action, and we have trusted only to rhetoric. If we are really to be a great nation, we must not merely talk; we must act big.

THEODORE ROOSEVELT,
26th president of the United States

We are Americans now, we live in the tundra
Of the logical, a sea of cities, a wood of cars.

> *MARILYN CHIN, American translator and poet*

We seek peace, knowing that peace is the climate of freedom. And now, as in no other age, we seek it because
we have been warned, by the power of modern weapons,
that peace may be the only climate possible for human
life itself.

> *DWIGHT D. EISENHOWER,*
> *34th president of the United States*

Being blunt with your feelings is very American. In this big
country, I can be as brash as New York, as hedonistic as Los
Angeles, as sensuous as San Francisco, as brainy as Boston,
as proper as Philadelphia, as brawny as Chicago, as warm as
Palm Springs, as friendly as my adopted home of Dallas,
Fort Worth, and as peaceful as the inland waterway that
rubs up against my former home in Virginia Beach.

> *MARTINA NAVRATILOVA,*
> *Czechoslovakian-born American athlete*

We travel by plane, oftener than not, and yet the spirit of our country seems to have remained a country of railroads.

JOHN CHEEVER, American novelist

I've been working on the railroad,
All the live-long day,
I've been working on the railroad,
Just to pass the time away.
Don't you hear the whistle blowing,
Rise up so early in the morn;
Don't you hear the captain shouting,
"Dinah, blow your horn!"

Author Unknown

America did not invent human rights. In a very real sense . . . human rights invented America.

JIMMY CARTER, 39th president of the United States

Where, after all, do universal human rights begin? In small places, close to home—so close and so small that they cannot be seen on any maps of the world. Yet they *are* the world of the individual person; the neighborhood he lives in; the school or college he attends; the factory, farm, or office where he works. Such are the places where every man, woman, and child seeks equal justice, equal employment, equal dignity without discrimination. Unless these rights have meaning there, they have little meaning anywhere. Without concerned citizen action to uphold them close to home, we shall look in vain for progress in the larger world.

ELEANOR ROOSEVELT, American first lady and writer

Though our challenges are fearsome, so are our strengths. Americans have ever been a relentless, questioning, hopeful people.

BILL CLINTON, 42nd president of the United States

The United States will never apologize for speaking or publishing the truth.

> *MADELEINE ALBRIGHT, Czechoslovakian-born*
> *American secretary of state*

Only America makes you feel that everybody wants to be like you. That's what success is: everybody wants to be like you.

> *ORNETTE COLEMAN, American jazz musician*

Whatever America hopes to bring to pass in this world must first come to pass in the heart of America.

> *DWIGHT D. EISENHOWER,*
> *34th president of the United States*

The United States is like a gigantic boiler. Once the fire is lighted under it there is no limit to the power it can generate.

>　　*EDWARD GRAY, Viscount of Fallodon,*
>　　*English statesman and writer*

In other countries, art and literature are left to a lot of shabby bums living in attics and feeding on booze and spaghetti, but in America the successful writer or picture-painter is indistinguishable from any other decent businessman.

>　　*From* Babbit *by* SINCLAIR LEWIS

I know America. I know the heart of America is good.
>　　*RICHARD M. NIXON, 37th president of the United States*

If there is any country on earth where the course of true love may be expected to run smooth, it is America.

HARRIET MARTINEAU, English writer

Things on the whole are much faster in America; people don't "stand for election," they "run for office."

JESSICA MITFORD, English writer

I found there a country with thirty-two religions and only one sauce.

CHARLES-MAURICE DE TALLEYRAND, French statesman

America is God's Crucible, the great Melting-Pot where all the races of Europe are melting and re-forming!

ISRAEL ZANGWELL, English writer and playwright

I leave you, hoping that the lamp of liberty will burn in your bosoms, until there shall no longer be a doubt that all men are created free and equal.

ABRAHAM LINCOLN,
16th president of the United States

This I know. This I believe with all my heart. If we want a free and peaceful world, if we want to make the deserts bloom and man grow to greater dignity as a human being—*we can do it!*

> *ELEANOR ROOSEVELT, American first lady and writer*

You can't separate peace from freedom because no one can be at peace unless he has his freedom.

> *MALCOLM X, American civil rights leader*

Liberty, when it begins to take root, is a plant of rapid growth.

> *GEORGE WASHINGTON, commander in chief of the Continental Army and 1st president of the United States*

Freedom is an indivisible word. If we want to enjoy it, and fight for it, we must be prepared to extend it to everyone, whether they are rich or poor, whether they agree with us or not, no matter what their race or the color of their skin.

WENDELL WILKIE, American lawyer,
politician, and business executive

Those who deny freedom to others, deserve it not for themselves.

ABRAHAM LINCOLN, 16th president of the United States

I swear upon the altar of God, eternal hostility to every form of tyranny over the mind of man.

THOMAS JEFFERSON, 3rd president of the United States

Injustice anywhere is a threat to justice everywhere.

MARTIN LUTHER KING JR., American clergyman and
civil rights leader

We must exchange the philosophy of excuses—what I am is beyond my control—for the philosophy of responsibility.

BARBARA JORDAN, American congresswoman and educator

Government is a trust, and the officers of the government are trustees. And both the trust and the trustees are created for the benefit of the people.

HENRY CLAY, American statesman

It is our glory that whilst other nations have extended their dominions by the sword we have never acquired any territory except by fair purchase or, as in the case of Texas, by the voluntary determination of a brave, kindred, and independent people to blend their destinies with our own.

JAMES BUCHANAN, 15th president of the United States

Lives of great men all remind us
We can make our lives sublime,
And, departing, leave behind us
Footprints on the sands of time.

HENRY WADSWORTH LONGFELLOW,
American poet and writer

I have a dream that my four little children will one day live in a nation where they will not be judged by the color of their skin, but by the content of their character.

MARTIN LUTHER KING JR.,
American clergyman and civil rights leader

More than an end to war, we want an end to the beginnings of all wars.

FRANKLIN D. ROOSEVELT,
32nd president of the United States

I only regret that I have but one life to lose for my country.
NATHAN HALE, American soldier and revolutionary

The peace we seek, founded upon decent trust and cooperative effort among nations, can be fortified, not by weapons of war but by wheat and by cotton, by milk and by wool, by meat and by timber and by rice. These are words that translate into every language on earth. These are needs that challenge this world in arms.

DWIGHT D. EISENHOWER,
34th president of the United States

I have not yet begun to fight.
JOHN PAUL JONES, American naval officer, as his ship
the Bonhomme Richard was sinking and
the British were demanding his surrender

The Revolution was effected before the War commenced. The Revolution was in the minds and hearts of the people; a change in their religious sentiments of their duties and obligations.

JOHN ADAMS, 2nd president of the United States

From the east to the west blow the trumpet to arms!
Through the land let the sound of it flee;
Let the far and near all unite, with a cheer,
In defense of our Liberty Tree.

THOMAS PAINE, Revolutionary patriot, philosopher, and writer

I can answer but for three things, a firm belief in the justice of our Cause, close attention in the prosecution of it, and the strictest integrity.

GEORGE WASHINGTON, commander in chief of the Continental Army and 1st president of the United States

We must learn to live together as brothers or perish together as fools.

Martin Luther King Jr.,
American clergyman and civil rights leader

That which in England we call the Middle Classes is in America virtually the nation.

Matthew Arnold, English poet and essayist

If there is any principle of the Constitution that more imperatively calls for attachment than any other it is the principle of free thought—not free thought for those who agree with us but freedom for the thought that we hate.

Oliver Wendell Holmes Jr.,
Associate Justice of the United States Supreme Court

Every American ought to have the right to be treated as he would wish to be treated, as one would wish his children to be treated.

JOHN F. KENNEDY, 35th president of the United States

The second day of July, 1776, will be the most memorable epoch in the history of America. I am apt to believe that it will be celebrated by succeeding generations as the great anniversary festival. It ought to be commemorated as the day of deliverance, by solemn acts of devotion to God Almighty. It ought to be solemnized with pomp and parade, with shows, games, sports, guns, bells, bonfires, and illustrations, from one end of this continent to the other, from this time forward forevermore.

JOHN ADAMS, 2nd president of the United States

I pledge allegiance to the flag
of the United States of America
and to the republic for which it
stands, one nation under God,
indivisible, with liberty and
justice for all.

FRANCIS BELLAMY,
American editor of the magazine
The Youth's Companion

Oh! say can you see, by the dawn's early light
What so proudly we hailed at the twilight's last gleaming?
Whose broad stripes and bright stars through the perilous
    fight,
O'er the ramparts we watch'd were so gallantly streaming?
And the rockets' red glare, the bombs bursting in air,
Gave proof through the night that our flag was still there;
Oh! say, does that star spangled-banner yet wave,
O'er the land of the free, and the home of the brave?

                  FRANCIS SCOTT KEY, American lawyer and poet

This American flag was the safeguard of liberty. . . . It was an ordinance of liberty by the people for the people. *That* it meant, *that* it means, and by the blessing of God, *that* it will mean to the end of time!

                  HENRY WARD BEECHER,
            American clergyman, editor, and writer

There never was a good War, or a bad Peace.
              BENJAMIN FRANKLIN, American writer,
                printer, statesman, and diplomat

God bless the Flag and its loyal defenders,
　While its broad folder o'er the battlefield wave,
Till the dim star-wreath rekindle its splendors,
　Washed from its stains in the blood of the brave!

> *OLIVER WENDELL HOLMES SR.,*
> *American physician, writer, and poet*

The loss of liberty to a generous mind is worse than death.

> *ANDREW HAMILTON, Colonial lawyer*

A man's house is his castle; and whilst he is quiet, he is as well guarded as a prince in his castle.

> *JAMES OTIS, Colonial lawyer and writer*

There is nothing wrong with America that cannot be cured by what is right with America.

> *BILL CLINTON, 42nd president of the United States*

. . . Whence came all these people? They are a mixture of English, Scotch, Irish, French, Dutch, Germans, and Swedes. From this promiscuous breed, that race now called Americans have arisen.

MICHEL-GUILLAUME-JEAN DE CRÈVECOEUR,
French-born Colonial writer

If there be any among us who wish to dissolve the Union, or to change its republican form, let them stand undisturbed, as monuments of the safety with which error of opinion may be tolerated where reason is left free to combat it.

THOMAS JEFFERSON, 3rd president of the United States

Let us have faith that right makes might, and in that faith let us to the end dare to do our duty as we understand it.

ABRAHAM LINCOLN, 16th president of the United States

O Columbia! the gem of the ocean,
The home of the brave and the free,
The shrine of each patriot's devotion,
A world offers homage to thee!
Thy mandates make heroes assemble,
When Liberty's form stands in view;
Thy banners make tyranny tremble,
When borne by the red, white, and blue!

DAVID T. SHAW, English actor and singer

We as a people have such a purpose today. It is to make kinder the face of the Nation and gentler the face of the world.

GEORGE BUSH, 41st president of the United States

Men make history and not the other way around.

HARRY S. TRUMAN, 33rd president of the United States

War should never be entered upon until every agency of peace has failed. . . .

WILLIAM MCKINLEY, 25th president of the United States

The shadows that now lie dark upon our path will soon be dispelled, and we shall walk with the light all about us if we be but true to ourselves as we have wished to be known in the counsels of the world and in the thoughts of all those who love liberty and justice and the right exalted.

WOODROW WILSON, 28th president of the United States

The life of a man is three-score years and ten: a little more, a little less. The life of a nation is the fullness of the measure of its will to live.

FRANKLIN D. ROOSEVELT,
32nd president of the United States

My friends, we live in a world that is hit by lightning. So much is changing and will change, but so much endures, and transcends time.

RONALD REAGAN, 40th president of the United States

The peoples of the earth face the future with grave uncertainty, composed almost equally of great hopes and great fears. In this time of doubt, they look to the United States as never before for good will, strength, and wise leadership.

HARRY S. TRUMAN, 33rd president of the United States

With a new vision of government, a new sense of responsibility, a new spirit of community, we will sustain America's journey. The promise we sought in a new land we will find again in a land of new promise.

BILL CLINTON, 42nd president of the United States

What you do is as important as anything government does.

GEORGE W. BUSH, 43rd president of the United States

With malice toward none, with charity for all, with firmness in the right as God gives us to see the right, let us strive on to finish the work we are in, to bind up the nation's wounds, to care for him who shall have borne the battle and for his widow and his orphan, to do all which may achieve and cherish a just and lasting peace among ourselves and with all nations.

ABRAHAM LINCOLN,
16th president of the United States